War Room Strategies

Developing Effectual Prayers for God's Glory

Michelle Stimpson

TABLE OF CONTENTS

INTRODUCTION

As for me, far be it from me that I should sin against the Lord by failing to pray for you....

1 Samuel 12:23

There's a lot of *talk* about prayer, but many believers feel ill-equipped to actually *do* the praying we know needs to happen. Consequently, our prayers often sound like, "God, help _____ to have a good day. In Jesus' name. Amen."

All prayer to God is good. We are informed, however, in James 5:16 that the "effectual fervent prayer of a righteous man availeth much." If we read that portion of scripture too quickly, it might seem that when a person prays with their whole heart, it will be effective. But that's not how the scripture reads. The prayer itself must be effective (aimed at producing the result wanted or needed) and fervent (heartfelt and sincere) as a *prerequisite* to availing. It is effective *ahead* of time. It works because it is in line with God's will, and God always honors the prayers of the righteous in Christ who seek to honor Him.

That said, we must take our eyes off of ourselves when we pray. Prayers aimed at making our lives more convenient, making others treat us a certain way, or satisfying the desires of the flesh are misaligned (James 4:3). Though the prayers may not be completely outside of the realm of what is "good" or God's desire, they are, at heart, self-centered.

The only way to pray confidently and with expectancy (i.e. effectually) is to pray sincerely as Jesus taught. Our prayers as believers who have had the keys to the Kingdom returned to us through the blood of Christ are to be as holy as the very prayers of Jesus. His prayers—in fact His entire life—were dedicated to seeing God's rule and glory on earth as it is in heaven.

Those who are exclusively dedicated to seeing God's plans and ways manifest on earth can pray effectually and fervently. Their desires and their hearts are in proper position. It seems odd in a time when there is so much preaching and teaching on God's goodness and His grace to put a condition on prayer. After all, He has been known to confound the wise and learned by answering the prayers of the weak. He's good like that and meets us exactly where we are and builds us up from there. There really is no wrong way to pray because, at least, we acknowledge in faith who He is in prayer, and He does listen to His own (Proverbs 15:29).

But let's say a misguided Christian woman is praying for a certain man to become her husband. However, the man is already married to another woman. This single woman is praying outside of the will of God. The Lord still loves her, but it would be against His character to fulfill her request. God does not operate against Himself.

Perhaps there's a Christian lady who has grown up adhering to the zodiac signs. She is a Pisces who is having trouble with a boss at her job, whom she knows is a Gemini. She prays and asks God to give her a boss who is a Taurus because Pisces and Taurus zodiac signs always get along. This prayer is a mixture of two different belief systems. God, the Creator of stars, is not ruled by them. The prayer may be fervent, but it is not effectual because it does not align with the God of all galaxies.

Or let's say, there's a man who is praying for a better job and more money. He's praying fervently every night, touching and agreeing with other believers, looking up and quoting scriptures, and he even faithfully fasts twice a week. It seems good and right to request more from our generous heavenly Father.

However, if this same man is already mismanaging what God has given him and really only wants more money so that he can brag around his twin brother, this man's motives are amiss. Until he receives wisdom for stewarding a small amount of money, he will only make bigger mistakes with larger amounts of money (Luke 16:10). Furthermore, his desire to create envy in his brother is not from God. This man can try to cover his motives with churchy rhetoric and even quote the scriptures that let us know God is actually *for* prospering His people, but the Lord knows a man's heart (Proverbs 16:2).

God is far too wise and too loving to set us up for disaster. He would much rather these two brothers remain allies than to elevate one, knowing the promotion would destroy their relationship due to the indwelling pride of this particular brother. So He does not respond to that prayer with more money at this time. Rather, He may arrange a set of experiences in the man's life that cause him to learn that money is not the answer to his problems and that his brother is one of the best friends he will ever know. Then, perhaps when the man's character can withstand a financial increase, God will honor that prayer for financial increase because he is ready. The extra money will be an addition to the greater blessing of a changed heart, rather than something that brings sorrow (Proverbs 10:22).

Finally, perhaps there is a family member who is terminally ill. We want that person to live because we don't want to go through the pain of not having that person here with us. But if that person is a believer who is satisfied with life and ready to return to our heavenly home, there is no need to pray that they will live on and on and on. Yes, Jesus raised Lazarus from the dead, but eventually Lazarus died again. Why? Because this is not our final destination. We are not meant to live here in this state of being forever. Believers, especially, should take comfort in the fact that this life is the shortest thing we will ever do. We have a great eternity ahead of us and it is God's will that we return to Him one day, though the transition may cause great pain for those left behind, in the meantime.

John 15:7 is perhaps one of the greatest comforts we can find regarding prayer. "If you remain in me and my words remain in you, ask whatever you wish, and it will be done for you." (NIV). When our wishes agree with His abiding Word, praying is simply a matter of agreeing with God and exercising the dominion He intended for us to have in this earthly realm.

It is hard to know God's will and His Word without knowing Him. Let Bible study and spending dedicated time alone with Him be your highest priority. No matter what your ministry, how many children you're caring for, or how little "free time" you have within a 24-hour period, I can assure you that you have all the time you need to do what *must* be done. Consider prayer a must. My big sister in Christ once told me that we can't "make" time for the things we want to do. No one has the ability to *make* more time. We have to "take" dedicated time for prayer from something else. These days, the "something else" is often television or social media. It could also mean stepping away from activities that aren't altogether damaging, but simply don't need to be on our lists of things-to-do.

"It is only in a life full of the Holy Spirit that the true power to ask in Christ's name can be known…Any thought of praying more and effectually will be in vain, except as we are brought into a closer relationship to our blessed Lord Jesus." (*The Ministry of Intercession*, Andrew Murray)

My prayer for you is that you will grow in the knowledge of Christ and the will of God as you develop prayers of attack and defense for your ever-growing circle of influence. The people of God are supposed to be the ones running things down here on earth in our Father's name. Let's get to it!

Confess your faults one to another, and pray one for another, that ye may be healed. The effectual fervent prayer of a righteous man availeth much.

James 5:16, KJV

I'm an educator both by profession and by gifting (Ephesians 4:11). As far as K-12 education goes, my specialty is teaching teachers how to teach writing. One of the first things I teach is how to help students organize thoughts into categories by using a graphic organizer. When you were in school, you might have called them by various names: Venn diagrams, flow charts, bubble maps, etc., but they're all useful for helping students wrap their minds around the scope of a topic. Before we can write, we need to know what to say.

Such is the case with effectual prayer. We have to know God's heart in order to pray strategically, in accordance with His will in heaven so that we can appropriate it in the earthly realm and resist the enemy. We need God-ordained plans to deal with our enemy, because he certainly has strategies up his sleeves. Priscilla Shirer explains in her book, *Fervent*, "If all we're doing is flinging words and emotions in all directions without any real consideration for the specific ways the enemy is targeting us and the promises of God that apply to us, we're mostly just wasting our time."

Now, if you're unfamiliar with the way the enemy operates, I recommend *Fervent*. If you're unfamiliar with your authority as a believer and what it looks like to operate in God's Kingdom and His promises, I encourage you to read Dr. Myles Munroe's book entitled *Rediscovering the Kingdom*. Through this book and careful Bible study, you will become more convinced of and familiar with your territory, your jurisdiction, and your authority as a believer. You will also learn the prayer life we discuss in this book is a part of what we enjoy after receiving Christ as savior. He is the way to the Father (John 14:6) and all that comes with life with God in Christ (Colossians 3:3).

This book takes a look at aligning our prayers with God's promises and our authority as believers as well as recognizing and casting down the arrows the enemy has trained on us.

Hear me in this: **Please do not limit your prayer life to what I share in this book.** The first part of developing a prayer (the **Prayer Strategizer**) has 10 sections. I encourage you to explore each section for as long as you feel led by the Holy Spirit to stay there. This strategy is not the end-all-be-all of prayer. It can only be an addition to what you already do in regular prayer and worship because God is bigger than ink, paper, and graphic organizers. This book gives one way of shaping your prayers, but it is not the Holy Spirit, Who is the greatest Teacher of all (John 14:26). He shows us how to pray even when we don't know where to start.

For example, when my daughter became pregnant before getting married, I knew she needed a certain prayer—one that I'd never had to pray before. I wasn't sure exactly what to pray. I only knew I couldn't base prayer on my feelings of disappointment, anger, or fear. I prayed in the Spirit for two days before I was ready to develop the graphic organizer. With His wisdom guiding me and reminding me of what I already knew by scripture, I was able to complete the organizer and pray effectively for her, my unborn grandchild, the child's father, and our entire family in a way that honored God—even in the midst of a situation that was not ideal. The result of the prayers inspired by the Holy Spirit and strategically created using this organizer brought about changes that could only be attributed to His goodness and glory.

One special note: You don't have to wait until something bad happens to start praying strategically. You can pray offensively or even for people you believe God is bringing into your life in the future. You can pray strategically for yourself, your family and loved ones, your co-workers, community, country, or a global cause. Use the **Prayer Strategizer** and the **Prayer** in conjunction with **The Watch** for any reason or concern for which you are called to intercession. The tools in this book are to be used to declare and stand watch as God's powerful words go forth!

Do not conform to the pattern of this world, but be transformed by the renewing of your mind. Then

you will be able to test and approve what God's will is—

his good, pleasing and perfect will. Romans 12:2

Start by naming and recording the start date of the battle. This is your official war declaration. Record the day you entered the battle strategically, because—until then—it wasn't really a battle. It was probably just a one-sided beat-down.

Consider giving the battle the name of a person or intended outcome. You may wish to tape a picture of someone or a list of the prayer partners who are joining with you in the war. Though space for an end date is provided, know that some prayers may be ongoing. It is also possible that some of your prayers may not come to pass until after you leave this life. That is to be expected, since you may be praying about something or someone up until your last day here. With a record of the battles on your heart, others can continue to pray and see God's Kingdom unfold even when you are basking in His glorious presence!

THE BATTLE:

_____

START DATE:

_____

END DATE:

_____

Spend as much time as you need on each section. Don't feel rushed to complete this strategizer in a few hours or even a few days. Proceed prayerfully, and be open to the fact that sometimes what we want isn't exactly what God wants. Where conflicts arise, always let God's thoughts take precedence.

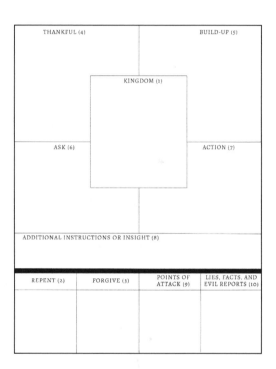

KINGDOM (1)

Jesus taught the disciples to acknowledge God's holiness and pray according to God's desires (Matthew 6). Though His thoughts are higher than ours (Isaiah 55:8-9, Ephesians 3:20), He has given understanding of the Kingdom's mysteries to those who follow Him closely (Matthew 13:1-17).

Prayerfully consider these questions as you seek to know God's desires for your situation or request:

- What would glorify God most?

- What outcome would be the biggest expression of God's love?

- Is there an example of God's heart on similar matters in the Bible?

- What did Jesus say/do regarding similar situations in the Bible?

- How will I know that God's will has come to pass in this situation in the earthly realm?

- In this box, also record scriptures that address the concern(s).

Like Abraham (Romans 4:19), a prayer warrior must learn how to "consider not" many things. DO NOT consider the following:

- How much you figure it would cost (in time, effort, or money) to accomplish God's will

- What has already been said, heard, seen, felt (emotionally or physically), smelled, or tasted

- How similar situations turned out for other people (or yourself) in the past

- The odds

- How far gone the person is at this time

- How other people may feel or think at this time

Record what you know (from your relationship with Him and scripture) will bring God glory and express His love. If you are not very familiar with the scriptures at this time, there are many free phone apps and websites that will allow you to conduct topical word searches so that you can find applicable scriptures. Also, consider asking someone in your church or prayer group for assistance in searching the Bible for specific verses to help discover God's heart for your concern.

At this point, we fall below the dark black line on the Prayer Strategizer. The black line represents the solid power of the blood of Christ. He is above all things.

So far as this situation or person has been negatively influenced by you, now is the time to repent of your part in the problem. Acknowledge unbelief and receive faith and forgiveness for that.

If you are unsure of how you might have contributed to the problem, ask the Holy Spirit to show you. Then, prayerfully consider the following:

- Have I spoken anything or acted in fear, pride, lust, envy, condemnation, frustration, etc., as it pertains to this situation/person?

- Have I offended? Have I deceived?

- Have I submitted myself to a worldly view of this situation/person?

- Did I fail to pray about this before now?

- Have I involved people who have no godly interest in this situation?

- Did I fail to follow God's direction regarding this concern?

- Did I allow myself to become intimidated or otherwise influenced by the enemy with regard to this concern?

- Have I enjoyed receiving pity or being viewed as "the savior" in this situation?

- Where have the lust of the eyes, the lust of the flesh, or the pride of life showed themselves in me with regard to this situation?

Write your responses and confess these things, agreeing with God that they were wrong. Receive forgiveness in faith, and then blot them out on your strategizer. You can cross them out with a line; use a marker to make those words invisible. Those words/actions are not to be repeated, recalled, reiterated, reviewed, or relived. The only exception might be a one-time recount in order to ask someone's forgiveness. In that case, be specific in your apology, so the person knows you are taking full responsibility for your actions.

Based on the integrity of His Word (Psalm 103:12, 1 John 1:9) you are forgiven, so abandon those things that were not in line with His will. This will be extremely important during **The Watch** phase.

FORGIVE (3)

Just as it is paramount your ungodly influence is forgiven and cast away, it is important that your heart toward others be pure as you move forward in prayer.

If you are unsure whether you're harboring unforgiveness regarding this concern, ask the Holy Spirit to show you. Then, prayerfully consider the following:

- Am I offended?

- Has anyone spoken anything or acted in fear, pride, lust, envy, condemnation, frustration, etc., and thereby, contributed to my becoming offended?

- Did someone fail me?

- Am I angry, hurt, disappointed, ashamed, etc., in reaction to someone else's words or deeds?

- Has someone slandered my reputation?

- Did someone try to intimidate, manipulate, or deceive me?

Write your feelings, confess them before the Lord, and cast those cares onto Him, for He cares for us (1 Peter 5:7). Blot out others' sins against you from your strategizer. You can cross them out with a line; use a marker to make those words invisible. Those words/actions are not to be repeated, recalled, reiterated, reviewed, or relived. The only exceptions might be within the context of seeking wise counsel toward recovery (Proverbs 24:6) or to discuss the offense privately with the one who offended you as you work toward closure (Matthew 18:15), if that is possible.

Based on the integrity of His Word (Ephesians 4:32), we are to forgive just as we have been forgiven. Abandon those residual feelings that were not in line with His will. They dissipate as we submit ourselves to pursuing God's will and resist reminders from the enemy (James 4:7).

If we want to know God's will clearly and assume our positions as the *righteous* ones whose effective, fervent prayers avail much, forgiveness is non-negotiable.

THANKFUL (4)

We're back above the line and ready to continue in agreement with His goodness.

What has happened already that you are thankful for? What is it that God has *not* allowed to happen before today that you can praise Him for right now? Record these things and scriptures in the Bible that correspond to promises of His protection, love, and provision for His people. You will add many more praise reports in the **The Watch** section!

BUILD-UP (5)

Where does your faith to pray in this matter need to be built? You may need to learn more or refresh your memory about what God can do and is already willing to do for His people.

17

For example, let's say you are being led by the Holy Spirit to pray for a particular job, but the person who is hiring for the position does not like you for reasons beyond your control. You might be tempted to say, "Well, I can pray, but if they don't want to act right, there's nothing that can be done."

Wrong.

Proverbs 21:1 (NIV) reads, "In the Lord's hand the king's heart is a stream of water that he channels toward all who please him." God has been known to change men's minds (believers or not) when they contradict with a believer who is intent on pleasing God.

When I first learned this, I thought to myself, "Isn't praying for people's minds and hearts to change kind of like trying to control people?"

No. It's like commanding Matthew 6:10: Your Kingdom come. Your will be done on earth as it is in heaven.

Many believers recognize that their loved ones have had their eyes darkened by the enemy and those who are in rebellion are acting under the enemy's influence, responding to his whispers and lies and deception. The enemy manipulates people and situations for evil.

What many believers have failed to realize is those same people can be influenced even more powerfully by love and truth. People are God's creation, not the enemy's. Praying for someone's will to line up with God's will is exactly in line with His thoughts. All the more reason to pray for them!

Furthermore, God has been known to circumvent natural laws in order to accomplish His goals for His people. He made an axhead float on water (2 Kings 6:1-7), He made one day last longer than any other (Joshua 10:13), and Jesus raised people from the dead (John 11:38-44).

As a believer who is settled on the authority of God's Word, recognize that He is able. Make note of the miraculous things that have already happened in your life. Recall the testimonies of other believers who have experienced divine intervention. Then record scriptures that will build your faith in this matter as well, because we tend to ask and receive according to our faith.

Ask (6)

Ask for whatever is lacking in this situation, whether it be wisdom, maturity, favor, finances, etc.

This section is especially important if you are praying for someone who is lost or in rebellion. You can ask for mercy and favor on their behalf even though they are not acting in accordance with God's will at the time. Knowing that Peter would betray Him and fall into fear, Jesus prayed Peter's faith would not fail him (Luke 22:32). The enemy wanted to take *everything* from Peter, but Jesus prayed the results of Peter's sin would not cause him to be lost forever.

Likewise, if you have a loved one who is currently involved in a lifestyle that could lead to devastating disease or a damaged court record, you can pray for mercy even now. You can pray the traps the enemy has set for them in their rebellion be foiled, so when they do turn back to God, they will not look like what they've suffered through.

God certainly has consequences for sin. Like any loving parent who corrects a child with consequences, that correction is intended to be a wake-up call to remind them they are acting outside of what they're called to be. There is godly correction.

But the enemy wants to tack on *even more* consequences, because he's just evil like that. Stand up to him. Let him know he will do no more than what God's loving correction allows.

19

Record specific requests. Then search and record scriptures that answer those requests.

ACTION (7)

The Word lets us know that faith without works is dead (James 2:14-19). More good news: God has promised His people that He would cause us to will and *do* what pleases Him (Ezekiel 36:26-27, Philippians 2:13).

For this section, seek and record His direction for what you need to do in accordance with His will. Prayerfully consider these questions:

- What does God want me to do at this time?

- Do I need to just be still?

- Do I need to make a sacrifice of time, effort, and/or money?

- Do I need to say anything or be quiet?

Then, wait on His guidance. If you receive no directive immediately, do nothing except continue to pray. (I don't even let people know that I'm warring on their behalf if they're still fighting for the other team.)

Our prayers often serve as the prerequisite to action, preparing people's hearts and arranging circumstances so that when/if you are called to action, everything is in place for victory. So don't be surprised if your main "action" or only "action" is prayer. It wouldn't be the first time someone stood still in faith and watched the Lord fight the battle.

If God reveals specific action in addition to prayer, record those required actions and scriptures that will edify you as you go forth. Consider including a checkbox for each action item, if appropriate.

ADDITIONAL INSTRUCTION OR INSIGHT (8)

Record more wisdom from the Holy Spirit and confirm with scriptures.

POINTS OF ATTACK (9)

At this point in the **Prayer Strategizer**, we are back under the thick line. That's because now that we have a clear vision of what God wants in this situation, we can recognize everything that doesn't line up with His plan for what it is—evil from the pits of hell. Evil that is beneath the power of God.

Just like in the Garden of Eden, the enemy likes to slither in and speak lies to God's creation. Perhaps the only thing worse than a deceived believer acting on the lies of the enemy is for a clear-as-a-bell believer to stand by silently and watch it happen, offering no resistance.

As we consider several different aspects of what might be happening in a person's life, we can pray both offensively and defensively, covering them completely in prayer.

Prayerfully consider these questions as you complete this section:

- What outside sources are influencing this situation/person?

- What would block those outside sources?

- Is there something or someone that can be introduced at this important juncture to block the attack?

Believers must remember that we are not fighting against people. Rather, we are fighting against spirits (Ephesians 6:12) and a world that is hostile towards the things of God.

Record the sources of evil and write your counter-attacking words to those things. Also, record scriptures to counter the voices.

For example, if I were completing this strategizer for a troubled nephew who is involved with the wrong crowd, the Holy Spirit might identify the voices of influence coming from his friends and celebrities he follows, as well as from his past. I might write in the section for **Points of Attack**:

- Past hurts/pains/rejection

- Broken relationship with father

- Friends at work who are just as lost

- Ungodly influence in media

Then I would write: I silence the voice of the enemy speaking to my nephew and call godly influences into his life.

One of the scriptures I would be sure to record: He [The LORD] heals the brokenhearted and binds up their wounds (Psalm 147:3).

Of course, if this nephew were not a believer, I would ask the Lord to reveal Himself to my nephew and call him to repentance and salvation.

This section is for calling out everything else that stands against the glory of God as it pertains to this prayer concern. It includes reports, documents, physical substance, and sensory perceptions that are out of line with the Word of God. Additionally, lies and doubt that have popped into your mind about the situation/person need to be listed here. These sources of discouragement must be challenged.

There will probably be more of this type of false evidence that appears as you continue in the **The Watch** section, but for now just record what has already happened.

For many believers, this is where faith begins to wane. This is where many become double-minded and fearful. Doctors' reports, bank statements, and information from legal or medical experts can seem insurmountable. Facts are facts. We don't deny facts. We *face* facts and make them bow down to the authority of the Word of the one true, living God.

Facts *are* subject to change. But even if they don't change, the Word of God is still truth. I recently watched a Christian show where a man who had a stroke talked of the fact that even though his brain scans still showed nearly half of his brain was dead, he was fully functional. The man's doctor even admitted the patient's brain did not match his body.

The point is that you don't have to wait for a good report from someone else—you already have one from the Lord!

Record what has been reported. Write down scriptures that confirm the opposite.

Here is a sample of the completed **Prayer Strategizer** for the Warrior Wives' Ministry to which God has called me. I have scanned it so that you can see all sections. (I will blot out certain sections later.)

THANKFUL (4)

- my imperfect marriage (22+ years) and family - for Your Glory, God!
- all the technical, financial, presentation resources available now for THIS!
- the vision for this ministry

For we are His workmanship, created in Christ Jesus for good works, which God prepared beforehand that we should walk in them.

And God is able to make all grace abound toward you, that you, always having all sufficiency in all things, may have an abundance for every good work. 2 Cor. 9:8

BUILD-UP (5)

· I can do this!

Phil 4:13 - I can do all things through Christ who strengthens me.

Acts 20:24 - ...that I may finish my race with joy, and the ministry which I received from the Lord Jesus, to testify to the gospel of the grace of God.
◄ also

· God is putting the desire and the action in me! I receive it by faith.

"...for it is God who works in you both to will and to do for His good pleasure." Phil 2:13 also ►

KINGDOM (1)

· Wives will be @ our posts in power and prayer

Build strong families as part of the Kingdom Agenda

God recognized as our great source of love, life, and strength - praise for His MIGHTY acts and words and faithfulness to His people

· Also Ephesians 2:10

· The older women must teach the younger women... Titus 2:3-5

· We have the ministry of reconciliation (2 Cor. 5:18)

· God be merciful to us and bless us, And cause His face to shine upon us, That Your way may be known on earth, Your salvation among all nations. Psalm 67:1-2

ASK (6)

· The best platform for webinars/classes - need wisdom on this especially

· Partnerships/guests who will build the women who listen according to Your Word & way

"... that you may be filled with the [exact] knowledge of His will in all wisdom and spiritual understanding, that you may walk worthy of the Lord, fully pleasing Him, being fruitful in every good work and increasing in the knowledge of God." Colossians 1:9-10

ACTION (7)

Open my home for wives to meet - Fall 2016 ☐

Online webinars - late summer ☐

Launch website - " ☐

PRAY !!!

ADDITIONAL INSTRUCTIONS OR INSIGHT (8)

· Stop comparing myself to other speakers/Bible teachers - 1 Cor. 12:18 - "But now God has set the members, each one of them, in the body just as He pleased."

· DO NOT get sidetracked anymore - THIS is my primary assignment @ this time. Everything else is secondary (...let us throw off everything that hinders and the sin that so easily entangles... Heb. 12:1)

REPENT (2)	FORGIVE (3)	POINTS OF ATTACK (9)	LIES, FACTS, AND EVIL REPORTS (10)
- Procrastinating and being fearful of scrutiny - Mixing motives (ministry and business) - unwillingness to put myself "out there" and avail myself to my sisters Matthew 16:25 for whoever wants to save their life will lose it, but whoever loses their life for me will find it	· Older women who didn't do this for me - family - church - community	· Distraction (work, pressure from self to do "much more," worries about family), preoccupation with losing weight and hairstyles and fashion "Set your mind on things above, not on things on the earth." Col 3:2	- Who do you think you are to do this? ← see [counterfeit] Eph. 2:10 above - I have to play the "social media" games/tricks to build a "platform" - "God resists the proud, But gives grace to the humble. Therefore humble yourselves under the mighty hand of God, that He may exalt you in due time. 1 Peter 5:5-6

24

THE PRAYER

I call on you, my God, for you will answer me;

turn your ear to me and hear my prayer.

Psalm 17:6

Now that we are aware of God's will for the concern, we can pray effectually and fervently. Fervency comes from a sincere heart. Effectual prayers come as a result of praying in line with God's Kingdom agenda. From what we have here, we can formulate a powerful prayer that glorifies God, puts the brakes on the enemy, and grows our faith.

Use the scriptures and the revealed will of God as a basis for the prayer. By personalizing the scriptures to this situation, we appropriate His Holy purposes in the earth.

I suggest starting the prayer with the vision and scriptures from the KINGDOM section and continuing on through section 10, focusing mostly on the scriptures. There is no need to repeat what you have already repented and forgiven in sections 2 and 3, so stick to the scriptures only there.

Here is my prayer based on the **Prayer Strategizer** for the wives' ministry:

Abba Father,

Be glorified and recognized as our great Source of love, life, and strength. Be praised in all YouR glory, splendor, and might through this ministry to wives that You have given me. Let wives be found at our posts and families be raised up according to Your Kingdom Agenda in the earth. Be merciful, bless us, and cause Your face to shine upon us so that your way may be known on earth and your salvation known among all nations according to Psalm 67:1-2 through this ministry. Thank You for positioning my household and preparing this work beforehand, by Ephesians 2:10. I am blessed to honor Your command in Titus 2:3-5, teaching younger women and sharing the ministry of reconciliation given to us all in 2 Cor. 5:18. By faith, I receive the will and the do to complete what was given to me from the Lord Jesus. This I do by the life of Christ in me and You working through that holy indwelling according to Your words in Phil. 4:13, Phil 2:13, and Col. 3:3. Fill me with the exact knowledge and wisdom necessary to please You and make my life fruitful. I surrender and prayerfully receive as an answer to prayer, as did those before me in Colossians 1:9-10. All other weights, sin, and distractions be far from me as I press forward to fulfill Your call, per Hebrews 12:1. I command my mind to be focused on what You have given me to do and be occupied with heavenly pursuits by Your word in Col. 3:2. My life is Yours - let it be found in You according to Matthew 16:25. I humble myself before You that Your ways, Your agenda, and Your WORD be exalted through this surrendered life. Thank You for loving me and entrusting me, for training me, calling me, equipping me! I ♡ u!!! Be glorified now & forever!

In Jesus' name, Amen.

A few pointers about crafting your prayer:

- The Bible shows us that God calls those things that be not, as though they were (Romans 4:17). This gives us a powerful principle for prayer: Speak whatever needs to BE. So, instead of praying, "I pray that I can stop being distracted", pray, "I pray that my mind be focused and kept from all distractions".

- Prayer is not asking for anything that God has not already decided to do for and through His people. This prayer is simply an agreement with Him. You do not have to coerce God to be good. He's already good and infinitely better to natural fathers (Luke 11:13). Therefore, you can approach God boldly as a son or daughter.

- Putting God in remembrance of His Word by including scriptures honors Him (Isaiah 43:26). Repeating the Word causes us to hear His words again, which strengthens our faith (Romans 10:17).

- Remember to pray in Jesus' name. We are alive unto God through Him (Romans 6:11), so our surrendered will and prayer comes to Our Father as a result of the relationship through Christ.

THE WATCH

Be sober, be vigilant; because your adversary the devil, as a roaring lion,

walketh about, seeking whom he may devour:

1 Peter 5:8, KJV

THE WATCH	
Developments	Response/Resistance

In my opinion, this section is perhaps even more important than the previous sections. Many-a-Christian has prayed and spoken scriptures over a situation for hours on a Monday night, only to spend the rest of the week in doubt and fear because they came up against resistance. Remember that God Himself watches over His words to see that they are performed (Jeremiah 1:12). We watch and speak in agreement with Him, calling His will on earth as it is in heaven.

During THE WATCH—which can take days or even years as you are praying over children, perhaps—record the following developments along with their dates. Record your response or resistance to these events, which may be praise or new prayers and scriptures.

- Praise Reports – things that are happening as the Word manifests. You can either cross off sentences within the prayer as they are fulfilled, or add a few words so they become a point of thanks within the prayer if you'd like.

- Things to Cast Down and Resist – happenings, reports, words, actions, doubts, fears, and/or perceptions that need to be resisted. We are susceptible to what we fail to resist. Be aware of the enemy's schemes and tactics so that you can shut him down.

For example, when my daughter became pregnant, my first prayer for the baby was that it would be healthy. But when my daughter became very ill, it was clear to me the enemy was trying to destroy the baby by attacking the mother's health. The baby was healthy, but the baby's *carrier* was not. This was the enemy's back-door approach to my prayer. I began to pray over my daughter's health and it was restored. As you continue in prayer, add these boxes to the prayer: (Psalm 91 is a chapter that covers protection for your entire "tent". I claimed those scriptures in the second column.)

- Word of Wisdom – if you receive a word of wisdom or prophecy that you wish to record, test, and confirm with scripture, use these rows.

- Additional Insight – anything else that you become aware of during THE WATCH can be recorded and addressed through the scriptures in the response section. This could include offensive maneuvers, declaring and commanding *before* the enemy has an opportunity to get a foothold in the situation. The more you watch and pray, the more you'll be able to anticipate the enemy's schemes. He has been outwitted by the Holy Spirit's revelation many-a-day!

If you have partnered with other believers, be sure to share these events as you are led by the Spirit.

A few things to remember:

- **Sometimes things *appear* worse before they get better.** The very people you're praying for may act out even more and say even uglier things after you start prayer for them. Expect resistance. If you're praying for your marriage to be restored and your spouse walks in the door and says, "I've decided I want a divorce," don't get scared, back down, and throw in the towel because of those words. Refuse to take offense because reintroducing unforgiveness gives the enemy the upper hand (2 Corinthians 2:10-11). Simply record this event in THE WATCH and address it with the Word. I would even blot out those words so that they could easily slip from my memory and I could focus on the resistance instead.

  Remember: This is a WAR! You are reclaiming enemy territory. Our adversary will not go down without a fight...but he *will* go down! Aside from seeing your prayers answered and God glorified, you will get the reward of wholeness, maturity and nothing lacking (James 1:2-8) for standing through this test of your faith. *This* is how mature believers are built.

- **DO NOT ACT, SPEAK, or allow yourself to ENTERTAIN THOUGHTS outside of your agreement with God's Word.** I can't even begin to tell you how important this is. During **The Watch**, you are on guard, resisting things that come against your prayer. Guards do not open the gate for an enemy. Guards do not play patty-cake with an enemy at the gate. Guards do not fall asleep on their jobs. In short, guards do not annul their own prayers by disagreeing with God, nor do they abandon their posts when opposition comes. Just because the enemy *approaches* you doesn't mean he can *overcome* you. Stay submitted to God. Stand. Resist. Watch the enemy flee (James 4:7).

You need to be especially thoughtful with your word choice. Suppose you are praying for healing and someone asks, "How have you been feeling lately?" Perhaps your body actually feels like a bowl of wet noodles, but you've been speaking that you are healed. Don't respond, "I feel terrible! My body is so lame! This has been going on for two weeks already! Just pray for me, sister."

No. All that does is shoot down your faith and theirs, too, not to mention rolling out the welcome mat for the enemy to use your words against you. After all, *we* are the ones with the power of life and death in our tongues (Proverbs 18:21).

Instead, consider responding with the truth rather than facts and lying symptoms. Say, "I'm standing on God's Word for my healing through Christ Jesus. Continue to pray for me."

It has been my experience that many people are not asking such questions because they actually intend to join in the spiritual fight for your health. They're just being polite and making idle conversation. They mean no harm. But be aware that it's those small, seemingly "benign" conversations that catch us speaking words contrary to our own prayers.

Should you forget and accidentally say something contrary to your prayer (the Holy Spirit will let you know!), cast those words down. You can literally say out loud, "I rebuke those words and cast them into the sea," and continue praying toward your healing. No shame. No condemnation. Just move forward and ask the Holy Spirit to put you in remembrance of His Word, so you won't do it again.

Remember that you are being trained to walk with victory, endurance, and spiritual maturity through this process. You will see and know God in ways you've never experienced before now. THE WATCH is a *good* thing!

- **Pray as often as you are led to pray these specific words**. Some prayer warriors are led to pray the same words once or more every day. Others have specific days of the week dedicated to the particular burdens they feel on their hearts. The most important piece of advice I can share is to be led by the Spirit. There are times when I pray only what I'm covering in The Watch. Other times, I need to be reminded of the goal, so I review the entire **Prayer Strategizer** along with **The Prayer** and **The Watch**. During the most intense battles, I have been led to pray several times a day because the enemy is really trying to resist the Word. Again, the key is to be consistent and responsive to the Holy Spirit.

Following the prayer pages, you will find several blank pages for other prayers. Feel free to record and address additional prayer concerns on these pages.

STONES OF REMEMBRANCE

Bless the Lord, O my soul, and forget not all his benefits:

Psalm 103:2, KJV

Though we are constantly at war with the enemy, there will be points along the way where particular battles end. Use the Stones of Remembrance pages to keep a record of God's goodness and faithfulness to His Word.

THE BATTLE:
_____
Dates: _____ - _____

PRAYER PAGES

Table of Contents for Prayers

The Battle:

_____

Start Date:

_____

End Date:

_____

THANKFUL (4)

BUILD-UP (5)

KINGDOM (1)

ASK (6)

ACTION (7)

ADDITIONAL INSTRUCTIONS OR INSIGHT (8)

REPENT (2)	FORGIVE (3)	POINTS OF ATTACK (9)	LIES, FACTS, AND EVIL REPORTS (10)

THE WATCH	
Developments	Response/Resistance
Developments	Response/Resistance
Developments	Response/Resistance
Developments	Response/Resistance

THE WATCH

Developments	Response/Resistance

Developments	Response/Resistance

Developments	Response/Resistance

Developments	Response/Resistance

THE BATTLE:

START DATE:

_____

END DATE:

_____

THANKFUL (4)

BUILD-UP (5)

KINGDOM (1)

ASK (6)

ACTION (7)

ADDITIONAL INSTRUCTIONS OR INSIGHT (8)

REPENT (2)	FORGIVE (3)	POINTS OF ATTACK (9)	LIES, FACTS, AND EVIL REPORTS (10)

THE WATCH	
Developments	Response/Resistance
Developments	Response/Resistance
Developments	Response/Resistance
Developments	Response/Resistance

THE WATCH	
Developments	Response/Resistance
Developments	Response/Resistance
Developments	Response/Resistance
Developments	Response/Resistance

THE BATTLE:

START DATE:

_____

END DATE:

_____

THANKFUL (4)		BUILD-UP (5)
	KINGDOM (1)	
ASK (6)		ACTION (7)

ADDITIONAL INSTRUCTIONS OR INSIGHT (8)

REPENT (2)	FORGIVE (3)	POINTS OF ATTACK (9)	LIES, FACTS, AND EVIL REPORTS (10)

THE WATCH	
Developments	Response/Resistance
Developments	Response/Resistance
Developments	Response/Resistance
Developments	Response/Resistance

THE WATCH

Developments	Response/Resistance

Developments	Response/Resistance

Developments	Response/Resistance

Developments	Response/Resistance

53

THE BATTLE:

_____

START DATE:

_____

END DATE:

_____

THANKFUL (4)

BUILD-UP (5)

KINGDOM (1)

ASK (6)

ACTION (7)

ADDITIONAL INSTRUCTIONS OR INSIGHT (8)

REPENT (2)	FORGIVE (3)	POINTS OF ATTACK (9)	LIES, FACTS, AND EVIL REPORTS (10)

THE WATCH	
Developments	Response/Resistance
Developments	Response/Resistance
Developments	Response/Resistance
Developments	Response/Resistance

THE WATCH

Developments	Response/Resistance

Developments	Response/Resistance

Developments	Response/Resistance

Developments	Response/Resistance

The Battle:

_____

Start Date:

_____

End Date:

_____

THANKFUL (4)

BUILD-UP (5)

KINGDOM (1)

ASK (6)

ACTION (7)

ADDITIONAL INSTRUCTIONS OR INSIGHT (8)

REPENT (2)	FORGIVE (3)	POINTS OF ATTACK (9)	LIES, FACTS, AND EVIL REPORTS (10)

THE WATCH	
Developments	Response/Resistance
Developments	Response/Resistance
Developments	Response/Resistance
Developments	Response/Resistance

THE WATCH

Developments	Response/Resistance

Developments	Response/Resistance

Developments	Response/Resistance

Developments	Response/Resistance

The Battle:

_____

Start Date:

_____

End Date:

_____

THANKFUL (4)

BUILD-UP (5)

KINGDOM (1)

ASK (6)

ACTION (7)

ADDITIONAL INSTRUCTIONS OR INSIGHT (8)

REPENT (2)	FORGIVE (3)	POINTS OF ATTACK (9)	LIES, FACTS, AND EVIL REPORTS (10)

THE WATCH

Developments	Response/Resistance

Developments	Response/Resistance

Developments	Response/Resistance

Developments	Response/Resistance

THE WATCH

Developments	Response/Resistance

Developments	Response/Resistance

Developments	Response/Resistance

Developments	Response/Resistance

THE BATTLE:

_____

START DATE:

_____

END DATE:

_____

THANKFUL (4)

BUILD-UP (5)

KINGDOM (1)

ASK (6)

ACTION (7)

ADDITIONAL INSTRUCTIONS OR INSIGHT (8)

REPENT (2)	FORGIVE (3)	POINTS OF ATTACK (9)	LIES, FACTS, AND EVIL REPORTS (10)

THE WATCH

Developments	Response/Resistance

Developments	Response/Resistance

Developments	Response/Resistance

Developments	Response/Resistance

THE WATCH	
Developments	Response/Resistance
Developments	Response/Resistance
Developments	Response/Resistance
Developments	Response/Resistance

The Battle:

_____

Start Date:

_____

End Date:

_____

THANKFUL (4)

BUILD-UP (5)

KINGDOM (1)

ASK (6)

ACTION (7)

ADDITIONAL INSTRUCTIONS OR INSIGHT (8)

REPENT (2)	FORGIVE (3)	POINTS OF ATTACK (9)	LIES, FACTS, AND EVIL REPORTS (10)

THE WATCH

Developments	Response/Resistance

Developments	Response/Resistance

Developments	Response/Resistance

Developments	Response/Resistance

THE WATCH	
Developments	Response/Resistance
Developments	Response/Resistance
Developments	Response/Resistance
Developments	Response/Resistance

THE BATTLE:

_____

START DATE:

_____

END DATE:

_____

THANKFUL (4)

BUILD-UP (5)

KINGDOM (1)

ASK (6)

ACTION (7)

ADDITIONAL INSTRUCTIONS OR INSIGHT (8)

REPENT (2)	FORGIVE (3)	POINTS OF ATTACK (9)	LIES, FACTS, AND EVIL REPORTS (10)

THE WATCH	
Developments	Response/Resistance
Developments	Response/Resistance
Developments	Response/Resistance
Developments	Response/Resistance

THE WATCH

Developments	Response/Resistance

Developments	Response/Resistance

Developments	Response/Resistance

Developments	Response/Resistance

THE BATTLE:

_____

START DATE:

_____

END DATE:

_____

THANKFUL (4)

BUILD-UP (5)

KINGDOM (1)

ASK (6)

ACTION (7)

ADDITIONAL INSTRUCTIONS OR INSIGHT (8)

REPENT (2)	FORGIVE (3)	POINTS OF ATTACK (9)	LIES, FACTS, AND EVIL REPORTS (10)

THE WATCH	
Developments	Response/Resistance
Developments	Response/Resistance
Developments	Response/Resistance
Developments	Response/Resistance

THE WATCH	
Developments	Response/Resistance
Developments	Response/Resistance
Developments	Response/Resistance
Developments	Response/Resistance

The Battle of

_____

Dates: _____ - _____

Remember:

The Battle of

_____

Dates: _____ - _____

Remember:

The Battle of

_____

Dates: _____ - _____

Remember:

The Battle of

_____

Dates: _____ - _____

Remember:

The Battle of

_____

Dates: _____ - _____

Remember:

The Battle of

_____

Dates: _____ - _____

Remember:

The Battle of

_____

Dates: _____ - _____

Remember:

The Battle of

_____

Dates: _____ - _____

Remember:

The Battle of

_____

Dates: _____ - _____

Remember:

The Battle of

_____

Dates: _____ - _____

Remember:

The Battle of

_____

Dates: _____ - _____

Remember:

The Battle of

_____

Dates: _____ - _____

Remember:

The Battle of

_____

Dates: _____ - _____

Remember:

The Battle of

_____

Dates: _____ - _____

Remember:

 Michelle Stimpson, founder of Warrior Wives Club, is a national bestselling author, an educator, and a speaker who has trained thousands of women on everything from writing life stories to getting along with spouses. She has benefited greatly from the advice and wisdom of seasoned Christian women and is anointed to work with wives who are facing difficulties in marriage.

Michelle is a part-time educational consultant with an M.Ed. who uses her gifts and formal training to build the Kingdom for generations to come. Visit her online at www.MichelleStimpson.com or www.WarriorWives.Club.

If you would like to order another physical copy or get downloadable copies of

WAR ROOM STRATEGIES,

Visit

http://www.warriorwives.club/#!resources/c1sxh

Made in the USA
Columbia, SC
29 October 2017